THIS JOURNAL BELONGS TO:

_____

_____

Publisher: **ROYAL HAWAIIAN TOURS**

ALOHA
THE ISLAND OF:

FROM:

UNTIL:

Before I Go I Need To:

FLIGHT DEPARTURE

DATE	DEPARTS TIME/ AIRPORT	AIRLINE	CONFIRM#	GATE	ARRIVE TIME	AIRPORT

LAYOVER INFORMATION

| |
| |
| |
| |

CAR RENTAL

DATE: TIME: CONFIRM# LOCAL: COMPANY:

PICK UP:

DROP OFF#

PHONE#

FLIGHT RETURN

DATE	DEPARTS TIME/ AIRPORT	AIRLINE	CONFIRM#	GATE	ARRIVE TIME	AIRPORT

LAYOVER INFORMATION

| |
| |
| |
| |

CAR RENTAL

DATE:	TIME:	CONFIRM#	LOCAL:	COMPANY:

PICK UP:

DROP OFF#

PHONE#

HOTEL INFORMATION

HOTEL: _____ PHONE: _____

ADDRESS: _____

_____

CHECK IN: _____ CHECK OUT: _____

RESERVATION#: _____

HOTEL: _____ PHONE: _____

ADDRESS: _____

_____

CHECK IN: _____ CHECK OUT: _____

RESERVATION#: _____

HOTEL INFORMATION

HOTEL: _____ PHONE: _____

ADDRESS: _____

_____

CHECK IN: _____ CHECK OUT: _____

RESERVATION#: _____

HOTEL: _____ PHONE: _____

ADDRESS: _____

_____

CHECK IN: _____ CHECK OUT: _____

RESERVATION#: _____

Date _____ Today I: _____

_____

_____

_____

Points Of Interest: _____

_____

_____

_____

New Food Tried: _____

_____

_____

_____

New Friends: _____ **Contact Info** _____

_____

_____

_____

New Friend meet ups _____

_____

_____

Date _____ Tonight _____
_____
_____
_____

We Ate at: _____
_____
_____
_____

New Food Tried: _____
_____
_____
_____

Who Was There: _____ Contact Info _____
_____
_____
_____

After Dinner We Went: _____
_____
_____

Date   **Recap Of Today**

_____

_____

_____

Best Part

_____

_____

_____

Things I tried:

_____

_____

_____

Regrets:

_____

_____

New Friends: **Contact Info**

_____

_____

_____

What is Happening Tomorrow

Things To Remember

New Friends: Contact Info

Date _____ Today I: _____

Points Of Interest: _____

New Food Tried: _____

New Friends: _____ Contact Info

New Friend meet ups

Date _____ Tonight _____

_____

_____

_____

We Ate at: _____

_____

_____

_____

New Food Tried: _____

_____

_____

_____

Who Was There: _____ Contact Info _____

_____

_____

_____

After Dinner We Went: _____

_____

Date   Recap Of Today

Best Part

Things I tried:

Regrets:

New Friends: Contact Info

What is Happening Tomorrow

Things To Remember

New Friends: Contact Info

Date _____ Today I: _____

_____

_____

_____

Points Of Interest: _____

_____

_____

_____

New Food Tried: _____

_____

_____

_____

New Friends: _____ Contact Info

_____

_____

_____

New Friend meet ups _____

_____

_____

Date _____ Tonight _____
_____
_____
_____

We Ate at: _____
_____
_____
_____

New Food Tried: _____
_____
_____

Who Was There: _____ Contact Info _____
_____
_____

After Dinner We Went: _____
_____

Date   Recap Of Today

Best Part

Things I tried:

Regrets:

New Friends: Contact Info

What is Happening Tomorrow

Things To Remember

New Friends: Contact Info

Date _____ Today I: _____

_____

_____

_____

Points Of Interest: _____

_____

_____

_____

New Food Tried: _____

_____

_____

New Friends: _____ Contact Info _____

_____

_____

New Friend meet ups _____

_____

Date   *Tonight*

We Ate at:

New Food Tried:

Who Was There: *Contact Info*

After Dinner We Went:

Date   Recap Of Today

Best Part

Things I tried:

Regrets:

New Friends: Contact Info

What is Happening Tomorrow

Things To Remember

New Friends: **Contact Info**

Date   Today I:

_____

_____

_____

Points Of Interest:

_____

_____

_____

New Food Tried:

_____

_____

_____

New Friends: Contact Info

_____

_____

_____

New Friend meet ups

_____

_____

Date _____ Tonight _____

_____

_____

_____

We Ate at: _____

_____

_____

_____

New Food Tried: _____

_____

_____

Who Was There: _____ Contact Info

_____

_____

After Dinner We Went: _____

_____

_____

Date   Recap Of Today

Best Part

Things I tried:

Regrets:

New Friends: Contact Info

What is Happening Tomorrow

Things To Remember

New Friends: Contact Info

Date _____ **Today 1:** _____

_____

_____

Points Of Interest: _____

_____

_____

New Food Tried: _____

_____

_____

New Friends: _____ **Contact Info** ____

_____

_____

New Friend meet ups _____

_____

Date _____ Tonight _____

_____

_____

We Ate at: _____

_____

_____

New Food Tried: _____

_____

_____

Who Was There: _____ Contact Info _____

_____

_____

After Dinner We Went: _____

_____

Date _____ **Recap Of Today** _____

_____

_____

_____

Best Part _____

_____

_____

_____

Things I tried: _____

_____

_____

_____

Regrets: _____

_____

_____

New Friends: _____ **Contact Info** _____

_____

_____

_____

What is Happening Tomorrow

Things To Remember

New Friends: Contact Info

Date _____ Today I: _____

_____

_____

_____

Points Of Interest: _____

_____

_____

_____

New Food Tried: _____

_____

_____

New Friends: _____ Contact Info _____

_____

_____

New Friend meet ups _____

_____

_____

Date _____ _Tonight_ _____

_____

_____

We Ate at: _____

_____

_____

New Food Tried: _____

_____

_____

Who Was There: _____ _Contact Info_ _____

_____

_____

After Dinner We Went: _____

_____

_____

Date _____ Recap Of Today _____

_____
_____
_____

Best Part _____

_____
_____

Things I tried: _____

_____
_____

Regrets: _____

_____
_____

New Friends: _____ Contact Info _____

_____
_____
_____

What is Happening Tomorrow

Things To Remember

New Friends: Contact Info

Date _____ Today I: _____

_____

_____

_____

Points Of Interest: _____

_____

_____

_____

New Food Tried: _____

_____

_____

_____

New Friends: _____ Contact Info

_____

_____

_____

New Friend meet ups

_____

_____

Date　　　　_Tonight_

We Ate at:

New Food Tried:

Who Was There:　　　_Contact Info_

After Dinner We Went:

Date   Recap Of Today

Best Part

Things I tried:

Regrets:

New Friends: Contact Info

What is Happening Tomorrow

Things To Remember

New Friends: Contact Info

Date _____ Today I: _____

_____

_____

_____

Points Of Interest: _____

_____

_____

_____

New Food Tried: _____

_____

_____

New Friends: _____ Contact Info

_____

_____

New Friend meet ups

_____

_____

Date   *Tonight*

We Ate at:

New Food Tried:

Who Was There: *Contact Info*

After Dinner We Went:

Date   Recap Of Today

Best Part

Things I tried:

Regrets:

New Friends: Contact Info

What is Happening Tomorrow

Things To Remember

New Friends: Contact Info

Date _____ **Today I:** _____

_____

_____

_____

Points Of Interest: _____

_____

_____

_____

New Food Tried: _____

_____

_____

New Friends: _____ **Contact Info** _____

_____

_____

New Friend meet ups _____

_____

Date _Tonight_

We Ate at:

New Food Tried:

Who Was There: _Contact Info_

After Dinner We Went:

Date _____ **Recap Of Today** _____

_____

_____

_____

Best Part _____

_____

_____

_____

Things I tried: _____

_____

_____

_____

Regrets: _____

_____

_____

New Friends: _____ **Contact Info** _____

_____

_____

_____

What is Happening Tomorrow

Things To Remember

New Friends: Contact Info

Date _____ Today I: _____

_____

_____

_____

Points Of Interest: _____

_____

_____

_____

New Food Tried: _____

_____

_____

_____

New Friends: _____ Contact Info

_____

_____

_____

New Friend meet ups _____

_____

_____

Date   *Tonight*

We Ate at:

New Food Tried:

Who Was There: *Contact Info*

After Dinner We Went:

Date _____ Recap Of Today _____
_____
_____
_____

Best Part _____
_____
_____
_____

Things I tried: _____
_____
_____
_____

Regrets: _____
_____
_____

New Friends: _____ Contact Info _____
_____
_____
_____

What is Happening Tomorrow

Things To Remember

New Friends: Contact Info

Date _____ Today I: _____

_____

_____

Points Of Interest: _____

_____

_____

New Food Tried: _____

_____

_____

New Friends: _____ Contact Info _____

_____

_____

New Friend meet ups _____

_____

_____

Date _____ _Tonight_ _____

_____

_____

_____

We Ate at: _____

_____

_____

_____

New Food Tried: _____

_____

_____

_____

Who Was There: _____ _Contact Info_

_____

_____

_____

After Dinner We Went: _____

_____

_____

Date _____ **Recap Of Today** _____
_____
_____
_____

Best Part _____
_____
_____
_____

Things I tried: _____
_____
_____
_____

Regrets: _____
_____
_____

New Friends: _____ **Contact Info** ___
_____
_____
_____

What is Happening Tomorrow

Things To Remember

New Friends: Contact Info

Date _____ Today I: _____

_____

_____

_____

Points Of Interest: _____

_____

_____

_____

New Food Tried: _____

_____

_____

_____

New Friends: _____ Contact Info _____

_____

_____

_____

New Friend meet ups _____

_____

_____

Date _____ Tonight _____

_____

_____

We Ate at: _____

_____

_____

New Food Tried: _____

_____

_____

Who Was There: _____ Contact Info _____

_____

_____

After Dinner We Went: _____

_____

_____

Date   Recap Of Today

Best Part

Things I tried:

Regrets:

New Friends: Contact Info

What is Happening Tomorrow

Things To Remember

New Friends: Contact Info

Date _____ Today I: _____

_____

_____

_____

Points Of Interest: _____

_____

_____

_____

New Food Tried: _____

_____

_____

_____

New Friends: _____ Contact Info _____

_____

_____

_____

New Friend meet ups _____

_____

_____

Date   Tonight

We Ate at:

New Food Tried:

Who Was There: Contact Info

After Dinner We Went:

Date _____ Recap Of Today _____

_____

_____

_____

Best Part _____

_____

_____

_____

Things I tried: _____

_____

_____

_____

Regrets: _____

_____

New Friends: _____ Contact Info _____

_____

_____

_____

What is Happening Tomorrow

Things To Remember

New Friends: Contact Info

Date _____ Today I: _____

_____

_____

_____

Points Of Interest: _____

_____

_____

_____

New Food Tried: _____

_____

_____

_____

New Friends: _____ Contact Info _____

_____

_____

_____

New Friend meet ups _____

_____

_____

_____

Date _____ Tonight _____

_____

_____

_____

We Ate at: _____

_____

_____

_____

New Food Tried: _____

_____

_____

_____

Who Was There: _____ Contact Info _____

_____

_____

_____

After Dinner We Went: _____

_____

_____

Date   Recap Of Today

Best Part

Things I tried:

Regrets:

New Friends: Contact Info

What is Happening Tomorrow

Things To Remember

New Friends: Contact Info

Date _____ **Today I:** _____

_____

_____

_____

Points Of Interest: _____

_____

_____

_____

New Food Tried: _____

_____

_____

_____

New Friends: _____ **Contact Info** __

_____

_____

_____

New Friend meet ups _____

_____

_____

Date   Tonight

We Ate at:

New Food Tried:

Who Was There: Contact Info

After Dinner We Went:

Date _____ **Recap Of Today** _____
_____
_____
_____

Best Part _____
_____
_____
_____

Things I tried: _____
_____
_____
_____

Regrets: _____
_____
_____

New Friends: _____ **Contact Info** _____
_____
_____
_____

What is Happening Tomorrow

Things To Remember

New Friends: Contact Info

Date _____ Today I: _____

_____

_____

_____

Points Of Interest: _____

_____

_____

_____

New Food Tried: _____

_____

_____

_____

New Friends: _____ Contact Info ____

_____

_____

_____

New Friend meet ups _____

_____

_____

Date   _Tonight_

We Ate at:

New Food Tried:

Who Was There: _Contact Info_

After Dinner We Went:

Date   Recap Of Today

Best Part

Things I tried:

Regrets:

New Friends: Contact Info

What is Happening Tomorrow

Things To Remember

New Friends: Contact Info

Date _____ Today I: _____

_____

_____

Points Of Interest: _____

_____

_____

New Food Tried: _____

_____

_____

New Friends: _____ Contact Info

_____

_____

New Friend meet ups

_____

_____

*Date*_____*Tonight*_____
_____
_____
_____

*We Ate at:*_____
_____
_____
_____

*New Food Tried:*_____
_____
_____
_____

*Who Was There:*____*Contact Info*__
_____
_____
_____

*After Dinner We Went:*_____
_____
_____

Date   Recap Of Today
_____

_____

_____

Best Part
_____

_____

_____

Things I tried:
_____

_____

_____

Regrets:
_____

_____

New Friends: Contact Info
_____

_____

_____

What is Happening Tomorrow

Things To Remember

New Friends: Contact Info

Date _____ Today I: _____

_____

_____

_____

Points Of Interest: _____

_____

_____

New Food Tried: _____

_____

_____

New Friends: _____ Contact Info

_____

_____

New Friend meet ups

_____

_____

Date   _Tonight_

We Ate at:

New Food Tried:

Who Was There: _Contact Info_

After Dinner We Went:

Date   **Recap Of Today**

Best Part

Things I tried:

Regrets:

New Friends: **Contact Info**

What is Happening Tomorrow

Things To Remember

New Friends: Contact Info

Date _____ Today I: _____

_____

_____

_____

Points Of Interest: _____

_____

_____

_____

New Food Tried: _____

_____

_____

_____

New Friends: _____ Contact Info

_____

_____

_____

New Friend meet ups

_____

_____

Date _____ Tonight _____
_____
_____
_____

We Ate at: _____
_____
_____
_____

New Food Tried: _____
_____
_____
_____

Who Was There: _____ Contact Info _____
_____
_____
_____

After Dinner We Went: _____
_____
_____

Date   Recap Of Today

Best Part

Things I tried:

Regrets:

New Friends: Contact Info

What is Happening Tomorrow

Things To Remember

New Friends: Contact Info

Date _____ Today I: _____

_____

_____

Points Of Interest: _____

_____

_____

New Food Tried: _____

_____

_____

New Friends: _____ Contact Info _____

_____

_____

New Friend meet ups _____

_____

_____

Date _____ Tonight _____

_____

_____

We Ate at: _____

_____

_____

New Food Tried: _____

_____

_____

Who Was There: _____ Contact Info _____

_____

_____

After Dinner We Went: _____

_____

Date   _Recap Of Today_

Best Part

Things I tried:

Regrets:

New Friends: _Contact Info_

What is Happening Tomorrow

Things To Remember

New Friends: Contact Info

Date _____ Today I: _____

_____

_____

Points Of Interest: _____

_____

_____

New Food Tried: _____

_____

_____

New Friends: _____ Contact Info ___

_____

_____

New Friend meet ups _____

_____

Date _____ Tonight _____

_____

_____

We Ate at: _____

_____

_____

New Food Tried: _____

_____

_____

Who Was There: _____ Contact Info

_____

_____

After Dinner We Went: _____

_____

Date   Recap Of Today

Best Part

Things I tried:

Regrets:

New Friends: Contact Info

What is Happening Tomorrow

Things To Remember

New Friends: Contact Info

Made in the USA
Coppell, TX
16 February 2023

12884063R00073